SCIENTIFIC SURPRISES

by Sally Kindberg

GRAFTON BOOKS

A Division of the Collins Publishing Group

LONDON GLASGOW
TORONTO SYDNEY AUCKLAND

2

Icy Growth

When water freezes it expands.

1. Fill a small glass bottle to the top with water.
2. Carefully put the bottle (uncapped) into the freezing compartment of the fridge.

Later, you will see how the frozen water has expanded by the piece of ice sticking out of the top.

4

Electric Comb

don't let comb touch water

or it won't work

Water is attracted to static electricity.

1. Run a plastic comb briskly through your hair to build up a charge of static electricity.
2. Hold the comb near a thin stream of water.

The stream will bend towards it.

6

Ear Gong

fasten threads to coat hanger

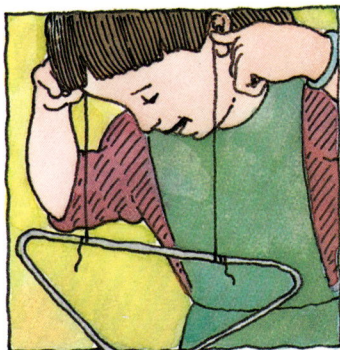

let hanger touch object

You hear sounds when sound waves vibrate against your ear drums.

1. Hang a metal hanger upside-down by two pieces of thread.
2. Hold one thread in each ear with a finger so that the coat hanger
    dangles in front of you.

Let the hanger gently touch another object so that it quivers. Vibrations
travel up the taut threads to your ear drums and make wonderful gong
music.

Dry Bottom

Air takes up space under water.

1. Crumple some paper and wedge it at the bottom of a glass or beaker.
2. Plunge the glass deep into a bowl of water.

When the glass is removed the paper will still be dry, because the water has been unable to force its way to the bottom. It is held back by air trapped at the bottom of the glass.

Egg with Poise

Salt makes water denser so that objects float more easily.

1. Watch an egg sink to the bottom of a bowl of tap water.
2. Then put another egg into a bowl of salty water.

The egg floats as the denser water holds it up, just as people float when they swim in the Dead Sea, which is the saltiest sea in the world.

Duck Displacement

The water level in a bowl rises when an object is put into it.

1. Mark the water level on a bowl half filled with water.
2. Put an object into the water and see how the level rises.

The object has pushed away enough water to make room for itself.

Whirling a Bucket

keep hat on just in case

If an object is swung round it is pushed outwards from the centre.

1. Put some water into a small bucket.
2. Whirl the bucket round and round quickly like a windmill.

You shouldn't get wet because the water will be pushed to the back of the bucket and won't fall out. (BUT TAKE CARE!)

16

Whack a Ruler

Air has weight.

1. Put a thin wooden ruler on a table so that about one-third of it sticks out over the edge.
2. Cover the ruler to the edge of the table with three sheets of newspaper (or even just one).
3. Bring your fist or a shoe down hard (WHACK!) on the bit of ruler sticking out over the edge of the table.

The ruler will break rather than lift up the sheets of newspaper, which are held down by the weight of the air pressing on them.

18

Fancy Flower

Plants suck up water through their stems.

1. Take a white flower and split the stem in two up to the middle.
2. Stand each half in two separate jars of water, each containing a different coloured ink or food dye.

After a few hours the white flower will have changed into a two-coloured one.

Leaky Tin

The deeper you go under water, the greater the pressure.

1. Make holes up the side of a tall empty tin – roughly the same distance apart – and cover them with sticky tape or plasticine.
2. Fill the tin with water.
3. When the tin is full, uncover the holes. (STAND BY!)

The streams of water from the holes at the bottom will be stronger than the streams at the top; the water at the bottom is being pushed out faster by the weight of the water above it.

21

Wobbly Walk

move arms about

An object or body has to keep its centre of gravity over its base, or else it topples over.

1. Walk along the top of a low wall.
2. Keep your balance by wiggling your outstretched arms up and down.

By doing this you are constantly altering your centre of gravity so that it stays over your feet at the base of your body.

For Emerald

Grafton Books
A Division of the Collins Publishing Group
8 Grafton Street, London W1X 3LA

Published by Grafton Books 1986

British Library Cataloguing in Publication Data

Kindberg, Sally
Scientific surprises.
1. Science—Experiments—Juvenile literature
I. Title
507'.24   Q163

ISBN 0 246 12818 6

Printed in Belgium by
Henri Proost